BEARPORT BIOGRAPHIES

TAYLOR SWIFT

SINGER, SONGWRITER, AND ACTIVIST

by Rachel Rose

BEARPORT
PUBLISHING

Minneapolis, Minnesota

Credits

Cover and Title page, © Kevin Mazur/Getty Images; 4, © Michael Tran/Contributor/Getty Images; 5, © Robert Gauthier/Contributor/Getty Images; 6, © Shuvaev/Wikimedia; 7, © Susan B Sheldon/Shutterstock; 8, © TJMSmith/Wikimedia; 9, © Rick Diamond/ACMA2013/Contributor/Getty Images; 10, © lev radin/Shutterstock; 11, © Jason Kempin/Staff/Getty Images; 12, © Tim Mosenfelder/Contributor/Getty Images; 13, © Everett Collection/Shutterstock; 14, © Kevin Mazur/Contributor/Getty Images; 15, © Jun Sato/Stringer/Getty Images; 17, © Royce DeGrie/TAS/Contributor/Getty Images; 19, © Bryan Bedder/Stringer/Getty Images; 20, © Featureflash Photo Agency/Shutterstock; 21, © Dimitrios Kambouris/Staff/Getty Images

Bearport Publishing Company Product Development Team

President: Jen Jenson; Director of Product Development: Spencer Brinker; Senior Editor: Allison Juda; Editor: Charly Haley; Associate Editor: Naomi Reich; Senior Designer: Colin O'Dea; Associate Designer: Elena Klinkner; Associate Designer: Kayla Eggert; Product Development Assistant: Anita Stasson

Library of Congress Cataloging-in-Publication Data

Names: Rose, Rachel, 1968- author.
Title: Taylor Swift : singer, songwriter, and activist / by Rachel Rose.
Description: Minneapolis, Minnesota : Bearport Publishing Company, 2023. | Series: Bearport biographies | Includes bibliographical references and index.
Identifiers: LCCN 2022038954 (print) | LCCN 2022038955 (ebook) | ISBN 9798885094054 (library binding) | ISBN 9798885095273 (paperback) | ISBN 9798885096423 (ebook)
Subjects: LCSH: Swift, Taylor, 1989---Juvenile literature | Singers--United States--Biography--Juvenile literature. | Country musicians--United States--Biography--Juvenile literature.
Classification: LCC ML3930.S989 R67 2023 (print) | LCC ML3930.S989 (ebook) | DDC 782.42164092 [B]--dc23/eng/20220816
LC record available at https://lccn.loc.gov/2022038954
LC ebook record available at https://lccn.loc.gov/2022038955

Copyright © 2023 Bearport Publishing Company. All rights reserved. No part of this publication may be reproduced in whole or in part, stored in any retrieval system, or transmitted in any form or by any means, electronic, mechanical, photocopying, recording, or otherwise, without written permission from the publisher.

For more information, write to Bearport Publishing, 5357 Penn Avenue South, Minneapolis, MN 55419.

Contents

Making Music History 4
A Childhood Dream 6
Stardom 10
Giving Back and Speaking Up 16
More to Come 20

Timeline 22
Glossary 23
Index 24
Read More 24
Learn More Online 24
About the Author 24

Making Music History

Taylor Swift smiled at the crowd as she made her speech. She had just won the 2021 Grammy **Award** for Album of the Year. Although Taylor had won this award twice before, this time was extra special. Taylor was the first and only woman to win the award three times.

Taylor won her first Album of the Year Grammy in 2010. At 20, she was the youngest singer to ever win it.

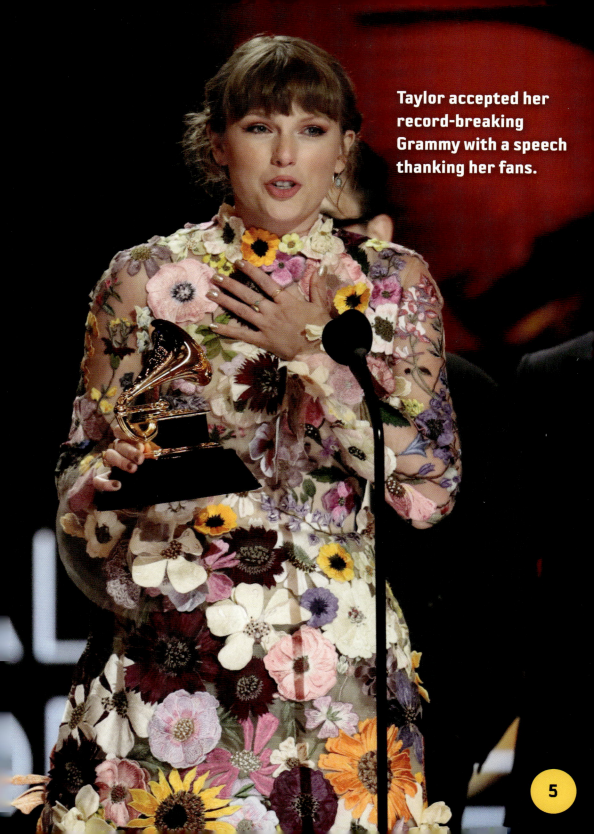

Taylor accepted her record-breaking Grammy with a speech thanking her fans.

A Childhood Dream

Taylor was born on December 13, 1989. She grew up on her family's Christmas tree farm in Wyomissing, Pennsylvania. Taylor loved working on the farm. She had an important job—picking bugs off the trees! When she wasn't capturing bugs, Taylor spent her time dreaming of becoming a country music star.

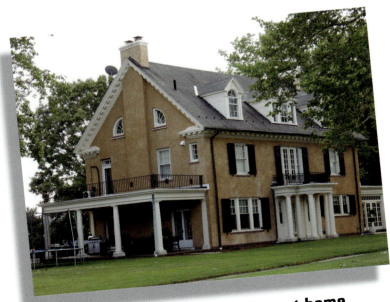

Taylor spent her early years at home with her parents and younger brother.

Taylor has called her childhood on the farm magical.

By age 10, Taylor was singing at school events and local fairs. Her parents did everything they could to support her. When she was 12, Taylor's father hoped a video of her singing might **impress** others. He sent it to many people, including the 76ers, Philadelphia's **professional** basketball team. Taylor was shocked when they asked her to sing before one of their games!

Taylor may have gotten her musical talent from her grandmother, who was an **opera** singer.

Taylor wrote a song called "Marjorie" about her grandmother, Marjorie Finlay.

Taylor with her father *(left)* and mother *(right)*

Stardom

Soon, Taylor began writing songs and learning to play the guitar. But it was hard to get **record companies** to listen to a young girl in Pennsylvania.

When she was 14, her family moved. They ended up just outside of Nashville, Tennessee, a city famous for its music. Before long, a record company wanted to make Taylor's music.

In 2008, Taylor wrote a song for country singer Kellie Pickler.

Before she got her big break, Taylor wrote songs for other musicians.

Taylor made her first album when she was 16—and it was a hit! The young country star used her songs to tell stories about her life, and fans instantly connected to her personal lyrics. Her popularity grew as more and more people heard her music. Soon, she was touring to **perform** at sold-out shows.

Taylor's first album, *Taylor Swift*, sold more than 5 million copies.

It turned out Taylor was just getting started. She wasn't willing to stop at just topping the country charts. Taylor started writing pop songs, too. Her next few albums were a mix of country and pop. Then in 2014, she made her first all-pop album. All the while, Taylor's fans loved watching her grow.

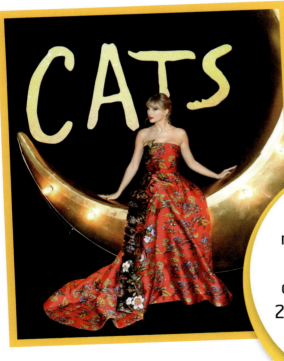

As she became more popular, Taylor wanted to show off other talents, too. In 2019, she acted in the film *Cats*.

Taylor puts on big live shows for her fans.

15

Giving Back and Speaking Up

With all her success, Taylor believed it was important to give back. She began visiting schools and children's hospitals.

Because music had such a big impact on her childhood, Taylor wanted all kids to have a chance at being musical. She opened a music education center in Nashville. There, kids learn to make music without needing to buy an instrument.

> Taylor often performs at concerts that help raise money for causes around the world.

Taylor opened her music education center at the Country Music Hall of Fame in October 2013.

Early in her **career**, Taylor worried about upsetting fans and so she kept most of her **political** opinions to herself. But in 2018, she decided it was time to tell the world what she thinks. First, Taylor **urged** her millions of fans to vote. Then, she began fighting for equal rights. Taylor decided to use her voice to speak up for others.

At the end of one of her music videos, Taylor asked fans to sign a **petition** in support of a law that protects the rights of **LGBTQ** people.

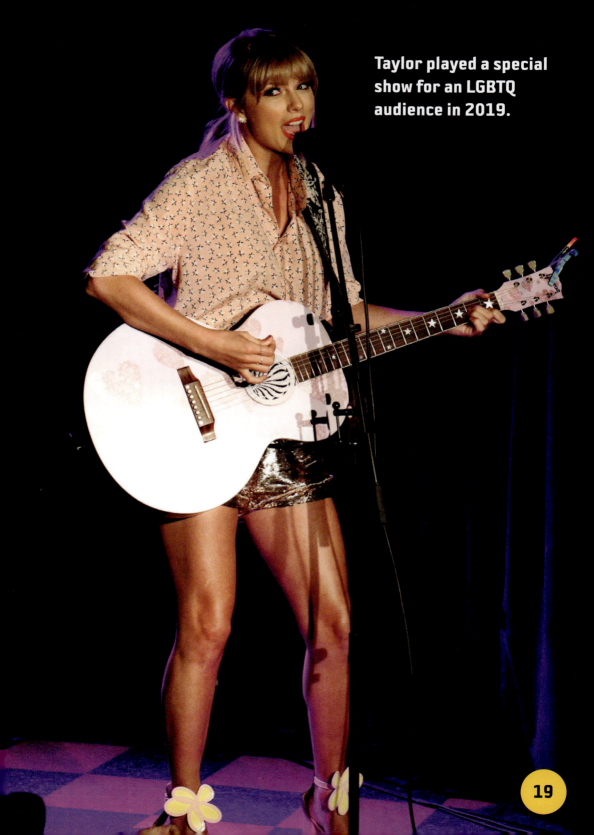

Taylor played a special show for an LGBTQ audience in 2019.

More to Come

Taylor started her music career at a very young age. With talent and hard work, she's won many awards and made music history. On her way to stardom she has helped people and learned how to speak up for what she believes. Taylor has already done so much. And there's more she still wants to do!

Taylor likes to keep her fans guessing. She often drops hints about what she's going to do next.

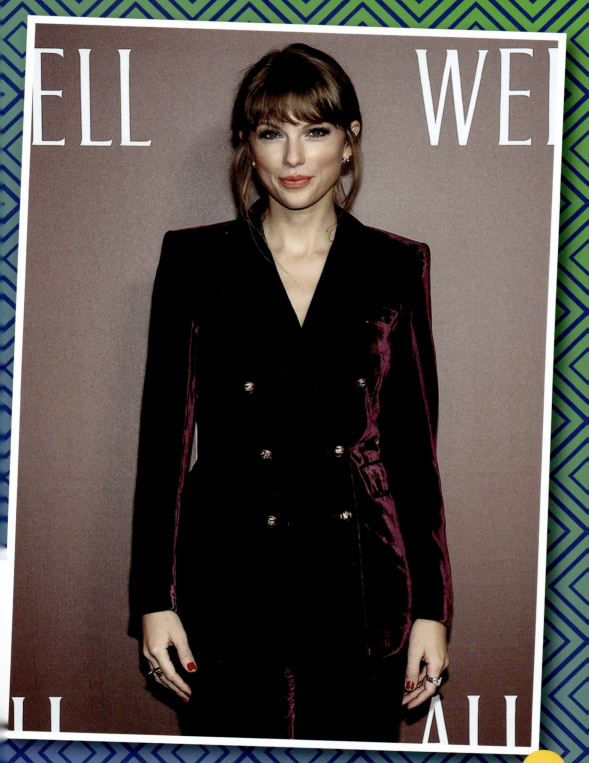

Timeline

Here are some key dates in Taylor Swift's life.

1989
Born on December 13

2003
Moves to Tennessee

2006
Makes her first album

2013
Opens music education center

2014
Comes out with her first pop album

2018
Shares her political voice

2021
Wins third Grammy for Album of the Year

22

Glossary

award a prize for being the best at something

career the job a person has for a long period of time

impress to make a person see the value of someone or something

LGBTQ lesbian, gay, bisexual, transgender, and queer; a diverse range of sexual orientations and gender identities

opera a play in which all or most of the words are sung

perform to entertain an audience

petition a letter signed by many people asking for a change

political the activities, actions, and plans that have to do with government

professional making money by doing something as a job

record companies businesses that make and sell music

urged tried to get someone to do something

Index

album 4, 12, 14, 22
bugs 6
causes 16
country music 6, 10, 12, 14, 17
education center 16–17, 22
farm 6–7
Grammy Award 4–5, 22
guitar 10
Nashville, TN 10, 16
political 18, 22
pop music 14, 22
Wyomissing, PA 6

Read More

Marx, Mandy R. *What You Never Knew about Taylor Swift (Behind the Scenes Biographies)*. North Mankato, MN: Capstone Press, 2022.

Olson, Elsie. *Taylor Swift (Checkerboard Biographies)*. Minneapolis: Abdo Publishing, 2022.

Learn More Online

1. Go to **www.factsurfer.com** or scan the QR code below.
2. Enter "**Taylor Swift**" into the search box.
3. Click on the cover of this book to see a list of websites.

About the Author

Rachel Rose is a writer who lives in San Francisco. Her favorite books to write are about people who lead inspiring lives.